Stan Rogers was one of Canada's best-loved singers. He wrote "Northwest Passage" in 1981.

"Northwest Passage" is a road song, a thoughtful trip across a vast land full of history. From behind the wheel, Stan connects the threads of many stories across space and time, following the footsteps of early European explorers as he contemplates their experiences.

Many explorers tried to find a route to the Pacific Ocean by following rivers through Canada's wilderness and by sailing the channels between islands in the Far North. Confronted by some of the fiercest winters in the world, these explorers repeatedly faced ice, blizzards and hunger. Inadequate technologies, scurvy and their belief in their own superiority over both nature and Canada's original inhabitants were perhaps the greatest obstacles they faced.

Some explorers made alliances with Inuit of the Arctic and the First Peoples of the Northwest Plains, but many failed either to make contact or to appreciate the fact that the people who already lived in Canada's North knew the land and how to survive on it intimately.

In the chorus, Stan refers to John Franklin, whose attempt to navigate a shorter route to Asia across the frozen Arctic archipelago in 1845 led to the loss of his two ships and the death of his entire crew. In the book, I tell the story of this ill-fated expedition — or at least as much of the story as we know today, for there are still a number of mysteries surrounding it.

I have chosen to illustrate the different threads of the song and to expand on the stories of the explorers. I have tried to show both Stan's inner and outer journeys across the country and to paint the enduring beauty of the changing Canadian landscape.

Stan didn't live to see ships crossing the Northwest Passage on open water, nor to comment on global warming or on the struggle of Canada's First Peoples to continue to live the way they choose on their ancestral lands. What a loss it is for us that we cannot hear him singing about what is happening in the world today.

For my Gramp, the late Ray James, and for my Gram, Norma James

"Northwest Passage" copyright © 2013. Words and
Music by Stan Rogers, Fogarty's Cove Music
Illustrations and commentary copyright © 2013 by Matt James
Published in Canada and the USA in 2013 by Groundwood Books

Groundwood Books / House of Anansi Press
110 Spadina Avenue, Suite 801, Toronto, Ontario M5V 2K4
or c/o Publishers Group West
1700 Fourth Street, Berkeley, CA 94710

The publisher would like to thank Dr. Bruce Bowden, Canadian historian, Fellow of
Trinity College, University of Toronto, for his helpful comments on the text.

We acknowledge for their financial support of our publishing program the Canada
Council for the Arts, the Government of Canada through the Canada Book Fund
(CBF) and the Ontario Arts Council.

Canada Council
for the Arts

Conseil des Arts
du Canada

ONTARIO ARTS COUNCIL
CONSEIL DES ARTS DE L'ONTARIO

Library and Archives Canada Cataloguing in Publication
Rogers, Stan
Northwest Passage / Stan Rogers ; as seen by Matt James.
Issued also in electronic format.
ISBN 978-1-55498-153-3
1. Northwest Passage—Juvenile literature. 2. Arctic regions—
Discovery and exploration—Juvenile literature. 3. Canada,
Northern—History—Juvenile literature. 4. Northwest Passage—
Juvenile poetry. I. James, Matt II. Title.
PS8585.O39533N67 2013   jC811'.54   C2012-900745-5

The illustrations were done in India ink and acrylic paint.
Design by Michael Solomon
Printed and bound in China

FSC
www.fsc.org

MIX
Paper from
responsible sources
FSC® C012521

Groundwood Books • House of Anansi Press   Toronto Berkeley

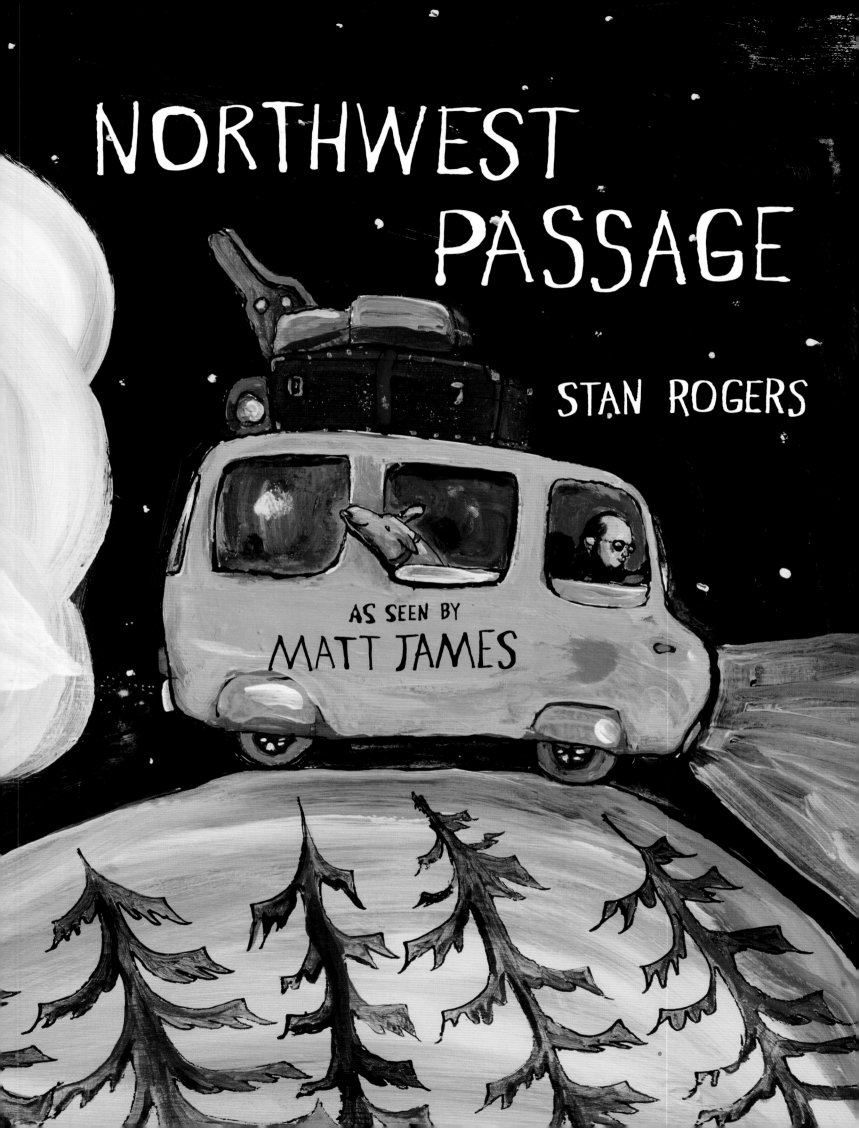

Ah, for just one time
I would take the Northwest Passage,

To find the hand of Franklin reaching for the Beaufort Sea,
Tracing one warm line through a land so wide and savage,
And make a Northwest Passage to the sea.

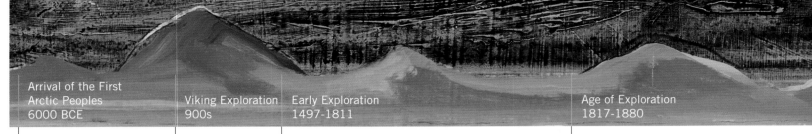

Arrival of the First Arctic Peoples
6000 BCE

People probably first came to the North American Arctic about 8000 years ago across a land bridge that then linked Asia and what is now Alaska. About 5000 years ago these people, who had learned to hunt and survive on the frozen seas and lands of the Far North, expanded eastward as far as southern Greenland and the coast of Newfoundland. They called themselves Sivullirmiut, or Tuniit, which means "first people." Later migrations brought fresh waves of people. The inhabitants of northern Canada are now called Inuit.

Viking Exploration
900s

Probably the first Europeans to visit the Arctic Islands were the Vikings, who may have reached Greenland as early as the late 900s. They traded with Inuit and named one of the islands "Skraeling," the Viking word for "indigenous people." There is a Viking settlement in northern Newfoundland called L'Anse aux Meadows that probably dates from the early 1000s.

Early Exploration
1497-1811

Much of the exploration of the Americas was due to the search for a passage between Europe and the riches of Asia that would be shorter than going around Africa or South America. In North America there were attempts on the Atlantic and Pacific coasts to break through the frozen seas of the Arctic. Much of the mapping, early knowledge and European settlement of the North American continent took place because of the fur trade. And a great deal of the exploration of northern and western Canada was done by people working for the North West Company and the Hudson's Bay Company.

Early explorers included John Cabot (1497), Jacques Cartier (1534-1542), Martin Frobisher (1576), Samuel de Champlain (many voyages between 1603-1633) and Henry Hudson (1609) from the Atlantic; Francis Drake (1579), Juan de Fuca (1592), Captain Cook (1776-1778) and George Vancouver (1792) in the Pacific Northwest; and Henry Kelsey (1690-1692), Sieur de la Vérendrye (1731-1743), Alexander Mackenzie (1789-1790, 1793), Samuel Hearne (1769, 1770, 1771-1772) and David Thompson (1797-1811) through the interior and rivers of northern Canada.

Age of Exploration
1817-1880

After the British defeated the French emperor Napoleon in 1815 and became the dominant naval power in the world, John Barrow of the British Admiralty declared that Arctic exploration, including finding a Northwest Passage and discovering the North Pole, was to be a British project. Underestimating how hard it would be to "conquer" the Arctic, the British government and its wealthy private citizens undertook many voyages of exploration. These voyages led to the mapping of the Arctic. The British were plagued by the cold, scurvy and lead poisoning in the tinned food they brought with them. Most of these explorers failed to learn from Inuit about how to survive in the Arctic.

The most important of these voyages were those led by John Ross (1817, 1829-1833), William Edward Parry (1819-1820, 1821-1823, 1824-1825), James Clark Ross (1829-1833) and John Franklin (1819-1822, 1826-1827, 1845-?). Up to forty expeditions in search of Franklin followed (1846-1880).

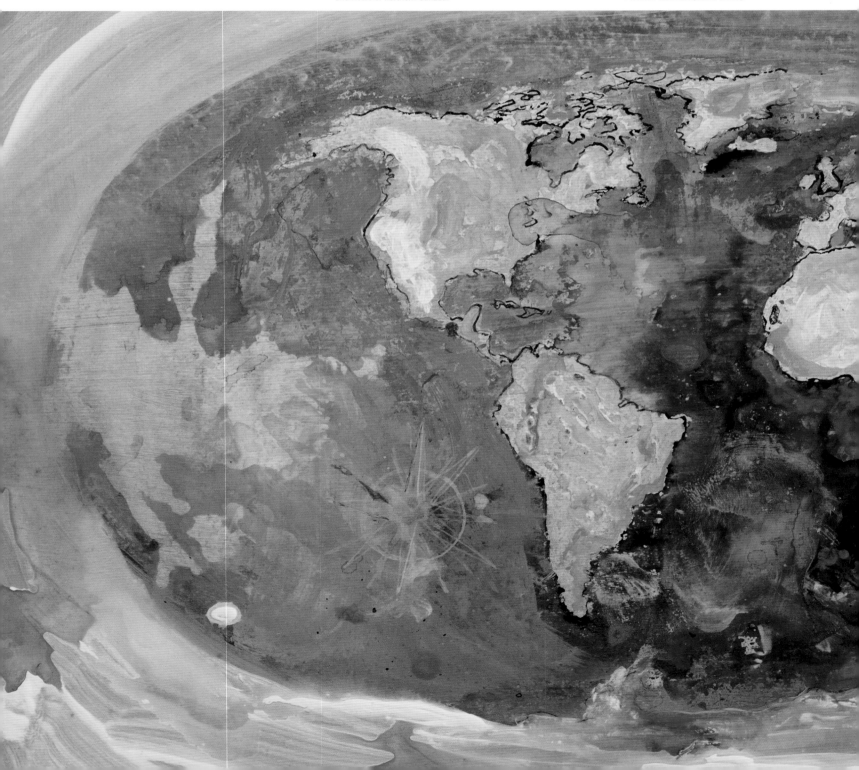

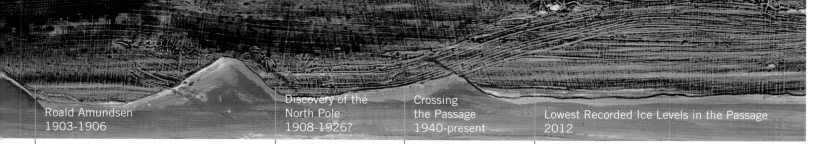

Roald Amundsen
1903-1906

Amundsen, a Norwegian, was the first person to actually navigate the Northwest Passage in a fishing boat called the *Gjøa*. It took him three and a half years (1903-1906). Unlike most of his predecessors, he lived among and took advice from Inuit in the region, wearing furs and eating local food that he hunted, thus avoiding freezing to death and scurvy. He also learned how to use sleds and sled dogs. The knowledge he gained on this expedition led to his being the first person to ever reach the South Pole in 1911.

Discovery of the
North Pole
1908-1926?

American explorers Frederick Cook (1908), Robert Peary (1909) and Richard E. Byrd (1926) each claimed to have reached the North Pole. There is substantial doubt about all of these claims. Roald Amundsen flew in an airship to the North Pole in 1926. His arrival was documented, and he may well have actually been the first to reach the pole.

Crossing
the Passage
1940-present

Henry Larsen was the first to sail the passage from west to east (1940-1942) and the first to sail from east to west in one year (1944). His boat was a wooden RCMP vessel called the *St. Roch*. Icebreakers began to use the passage in 1955, and since then shipping has increased steadily.

Lowest Recorded Ice Levels in the Passage
2012

Levels of ice in the passage have been decreasing steadily. Multi-year pack ice, the really solid ice that remains frozen for long periods of time, has diminished dramatically, even faster than climate-change scientists predicted. Today the countries whose lands circle the North Pole — Canada, the US, Russia, Denmark and Norway — are claiming that they have the right to control shipping through the passage as well as the minerals that lie beneath its waters. Species that depended on the ice, especially polar bears, and Inuit who used this space for hunting have been substantially affected. And some species of plankton and whales from the Pacific appear to have migrated to the Atlantic through the passage.

Westward from the Davis Strait 'tis there 'twas said to lie,
The sea route to the Orient for which so many died,

Seeking gold and glory, leaving weathered, broken bones,
And a long forgotten, lonely cairn of stones.

Ah, for just one time I would take the Northwest Passage,

To find the hand of Franklin reaching for the Beaufort Sea,

Tracing one warm line through a land so wide and savage,
And make a Northwest Passage to the sea.

The story of John Franklin and the mysterious disappearance of the ships and all the men who went on his expedition has always fascinated Canadians. Despite being one of the great failures in the history of exploration, Franklin has come to represent something about the bravery (and foolishness?) of the European explorers who tried to conquer Canada's Arctic. Franklin had previously explored mainland Canada and the Arctic unsuccessfully. This had convinced him that instead of relying on indigenous people and local food and warm furs, as some others had, he should bring everything he needed for the expedition from England. This included masses of tinned food; English china, glassware and silver utensils; woolen clothes and large libraries containing 1900 books in all. Expeditions to the Arctic usually had to spend at least one winter frozen in the ice. And explorers frequently fell ill to scurvy, a weakening disease caused by lack of vitamin C. The English were so impressed with their own technology that they were convinced, despite overwhelming evidence to the contrary, that tinned food would prevent scurvy.

When the ships set sail from England on May 19, 1845, many people came to bid the great expedition goodbye.

Franklin, who was considered at the time to be brave but not very brilliant, set out with 134 men in two great iron-clad ships, the *Erebus* and the *Terror* (which had already been almost destroyed on a previous expedition). He was supposed to explore a three-hundred-mile section of the passage that had not yet been mapped and which was believed to be the final link in the possible route between the Atlantic and the Pacific. It was expected to be an easy trip.

In July 1845 the *Erebus* and the *Terror* were seen north of Baffin Island by two British whaling ships — the *Prince of Wales* and the *Enterprise*. No European ever saw Franklin's ships again.

The red line on this map shows the approximate trajectory of the *Erebus* and the *Terror* as far as Baffin Island.

 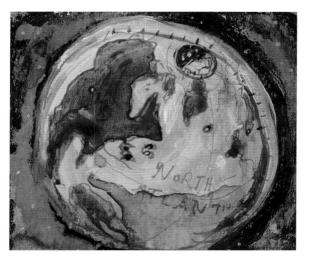

We know from a note later discovered in a cairn on King William Island that the first summer of the expedition (1845) probably went well. The sailors would have seen narwhals and walruses as they sailed between islands, pack ice and icebergs toward Beechey Island. From there they hoped to penetrate the unknown further reaches of the passage. And we can also be quite sure that Inuit observed the explorers sailing by.

Once winter came, however, it was normal for ships to be frozen in the ice for many months at a time. The men would read, play cards, write journals, eat their tinned food and drink the lemon juice, also carried in tin cans, that was supposed to prevent scurvy. Unfortunately their tin cans were sealed, very sloppily, with lead, which leached into the food and lemon juice and almost certainly helped to bring about their deaths. We also know now that lemon juice loses its vitamin C over time.

Sails were draped over the masts to keep the ship warmer. And sometimes the men would go out for short explorations of the surrounding ice.

When the ice thawed in spring 1846, Franklin set sail again. However three sailors who had died — William Braine, John Hartnell and John Torrington — were left buried on Beechey Island near what is today the Inuit village of Resolute. Chemical analysis of their bones and hair has shown that these men already had very high levels of lead in their bodies. But they died of tuberculosis and pneumonia.

Three centuries thereafter I take passage overland,

In the footsteps of brave Kelsey, where his "sea of flowers" began,

Watching cities rise before me, then behind me sink again,
This tardiest explorer driving hard across the plain.

Ah, for just one time I would take the Northwest Passage,
To find the hand of Franklin reaching for the Beaufort Sea,

Tracing one warm line

through a land so wide and savage,

And make a Northwest Passage to the sea.

By fall 1846, Franklin and his men reached the waters north of King William Island, the last open water they were to find.

Ellesmere I.

Bathurst I.

Cornwallis I.

Beechey I.

Devon I.

McClintock Channel

BAFFIN I.

King William I.

Simpson Strait →

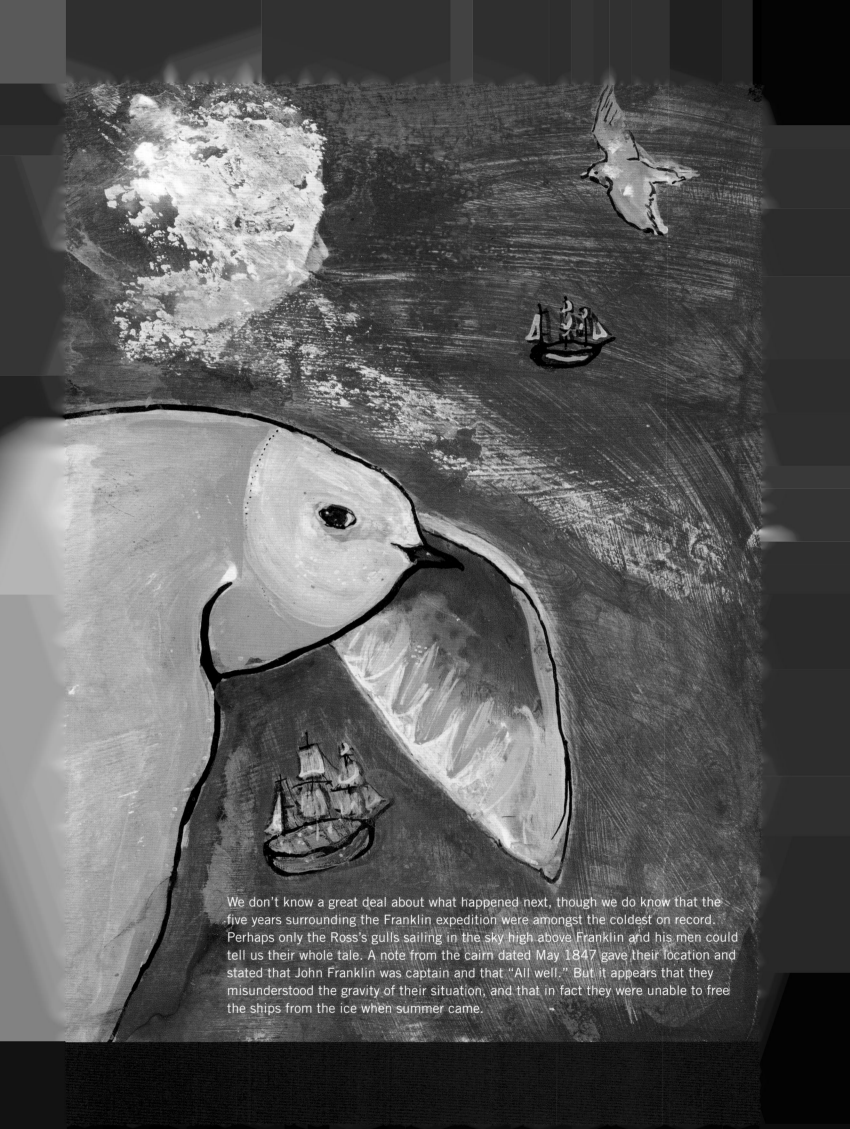

We don't know a great deal about what happened next, though we do know that the five years surrounding the Franklin expedition were amongst the coldest on record. Perhaps only the Ross's gulls sailing in the sky high above Franklin and his men could tell us their whole tale. A note from the cairn dated May 1847 gave their location and stated that John Franklin was captain and that "All well." But it appears that they misunderstood the gravity of their situation, and that in fact they were unable to free the ships from the ice when summer came.

And eleven months later, in April 1848, the same note was retrieved from the cairn by officers from the expedition. They wrote around its margins, saying that their ships had been frozen in the ice since September 1846 and that John Franklin had died in June 1847, as had nine other officers and fifteen men.

The note said that the 105 survivors were deserting the ships and heading out to seek the Hudson's Bay post, Fort Resolution, 1250 miles (2012 km) away.

Under the command of Captain Francis Crozier, they dragged along hugely heavy lifeboats weighing 1400 pounds (635 kg), loaded with tinned food, books, stoves, curtain rods, sponges, slippers and all manner of other supplies. The boats left deep ruts in the ice and snow that were later discovered.

They eventually threw away these supplies and abandoned the boats, in one of which two bodies were found by later expeditions. The boat was pointing back in the direction of the ships, suggesting that the men may have decided to return.

It is ironic that at this end stage of the expedition, as the men walked along the Simpson Strait, falling dead by the wayside one by one — some buried, some left where they lay — they were in fact discovering the last missing portion of the Northwest Passage.

According to Charles Francis Hall, an American who lived with Inuit from 1864 to 1869, there were Inuit eyewitnesses who claimed to have visited a frozen ship, seen men staggering around and dying, found evidence of cannibalism, and even encountered four men wandering on the island as late as 1851.

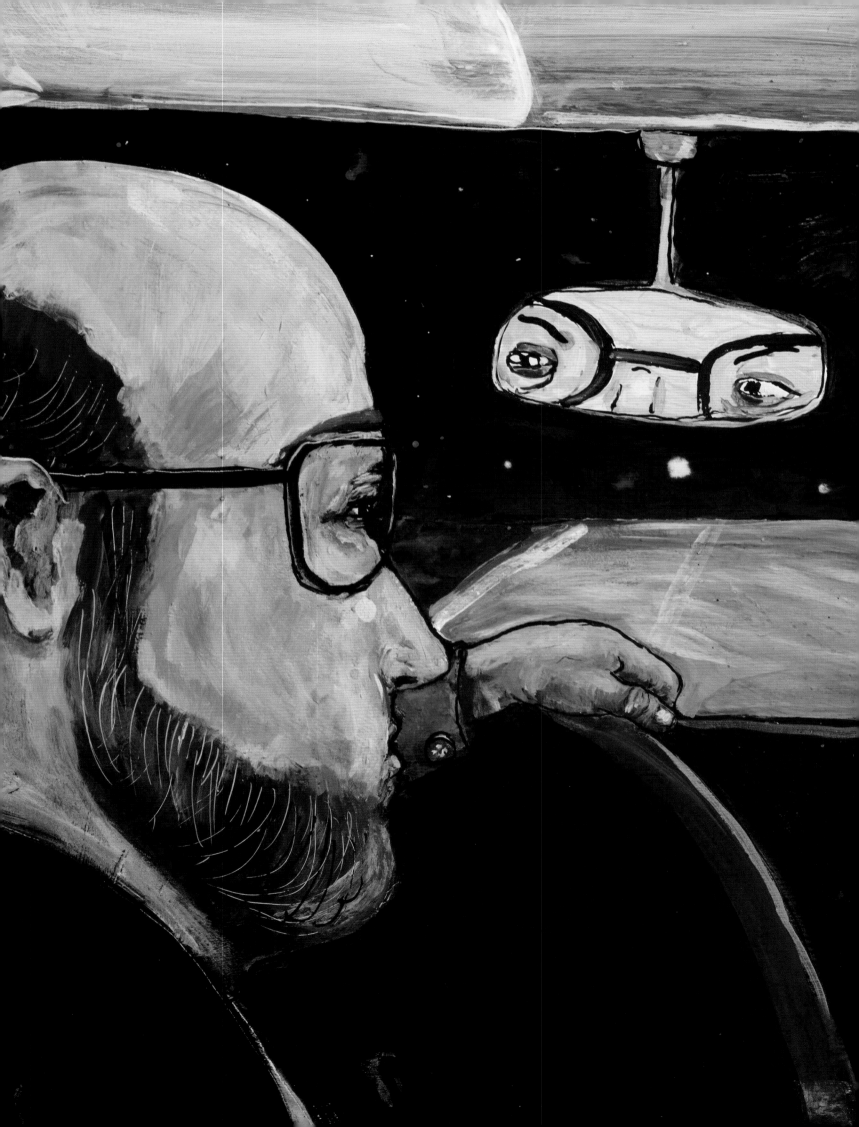

And through the night, behind the wheel, the mileage clicking West,

I think upon Mackenzie, David Thompson and the rest,

Who cracked the mountain ramparts and did show a path for me,

The great land mass of northern Canada was also a challenge to European explorers. Unlike Franklin, however, Alexander Mackenzie — the first European to reach the Pacific overland in 1793 — had the sense to rely heavily on First Nations people and to take their advice. With their help he was able to travel swiftly in huge canoes down great rivers — to the Arctic Beaufort Sea on what is now called the Mackenzie River, and to the Pacific on the Bella Coola River. Most of those who explored the land depended on the knowledge of their First Nations guides. Henry Kelsey was another European explorer who traveled in the regions of the Churchill River, Lake Winnipeg and the Saskatchewan River. His good relationships with First Peoples helped the Hudson's Bay Company become the predominant trading power in Canada.

To race the roaring Fraser to the sea.

Ah, for just one time I would take the Northwest Passage,
To find the hand of Franklin reaching for the Beaufort Sea,
Tracing one warm line through a land so wide and savage,

And make a Northwest Passage
to the sea.

Much of the mapping of the Northwest Passage took place as a result of the disappearance of the Franklin expedition. Lady Jane Franklin, Sir John's widow, and the British government financed close to forty expeditions in an attempt to understand what had happened. John Rae of the Hudson's Bay Company was able to speak to Inuit in 1854. They confirmed that the ships had been crushed in the ice and that the white men who had left the ships had starved to death. This news was confirmed in 1859 when explorer Francis McClintock discovered the note from 1847-1848 in the cairn. His conversations with Inuit confirmed Rae's descriptions of cannibalism, also described by Hall, and eventually people in England came to accept as fact what they had not wanted to believe — that the Franklin expedition had ended in a gruesome, tragic manner.

Nonetheless, a memorial was built in Westminster Abbey hailing John Franklin as the discoverer of the Northwest Passage.

Even today there is ongoing fascination with the disastrous Franklin expedition. There is a great deal of interest in trying to locate the missing ships, the *Erebus* and the *Terror*. The searches for them and the investigation of the remains of the members of the Franklin expedition have revealed the presence of massive amounts of lead in the tinned food that in its day was considered the most advanced form of technology. Now we believe that this reliance on technology instead of on the knowledge of those who inhabited the Arctic may have been an important cause of the disastrous end of the expedition.

And as climate change leads to dramatic loss of sea ice and the almost certain opening of the Northwest Passage to year-round shipping in the very near future, the countries that circle the Arctic are now trying to prove that they are the ones who should control access to the passage and to the vast mineral wealth under its waters. Thus Franklin, the Englishman, has now become a Canadian hero.

How then am I so different from
the first men through this way?

Like them I left a settled life,
I threw it all away,

To seek a Northwest Passage
at the call of many men,

To find there but the road back home again.

Ah, for just one time
   I would take the Northwest Passage,
To find the hand of Franklin
   reaching for the Beaufort Sea,
Tracing one warm line
   through a land so wide and Savage,
And make a Northwest Passage
   to the sea.

NORTHWEST PASSAGE

Chorus

Ah, for just one time I would take the North-west Pa-ssage, To find the hand of Frank-lin reach-ing for the Beau-fort Sea, Tra-cing one warm line through a land so wide and sa-vage, And make a North-west Pa-ssage to the sea.

Verse

West-ward from the Da-vis Strait 'tis there 'twas said to lie, The sea route to the Or-i-ent for which so ma-ny died, Seek-ing gold and glo-ry, leav-ing weath-ered, bro-ken bones, And a long for-got-ten, lone-ly cairn of stones. Ah, for

Three centuries thereafter I take passage overland,
In the footsteps of brave Kelsey, where his "sea of flowers" began,
Watching cities rise before me, then behind me sink again,
This tardiest explorer driving hard across the plain.

Chorus

And through the night, behind the wheel, the mileage clicking West,
I think upon Mackenzie, David Thompson and the rest,
Who cracked the mountain ramparts and did show a path for me,
To race the roaring Fraser to the sea.

Chorus

How then am I so different from the first men through this way?
Like them I left a settled life, I threw it all away,
To seek a Northwest Passage at the call of many men,
To find there but the road back home again.

Chorus

And it will be I'll come again to loved ones left at home,
Place the journals on the mantel, bake the frost out of my bones,
Leaving memories far behind me, only memories after all,
And hardships then, the hardest to recall.

Chorus

Sir Humphrey Gilbert (1539-1583)

Sir Humphrey Gilbert was one of a group of men around the time of Elizabeth I who were trying to understand how the New World could be put to the service of England. They believed that there was a way to reach Asia, probably through a Northwest Passage. But their knowledge of the actual geography was still very weak. Gilbert made a number of trips to the continent on his tiny ship, the *Squirrel*, finally reaching Newfoundland in 1583 and claiming the island for England on August 5.

Samuel de Champlain (c1570-1635)

Champlain, serving the interests of the French Crown and its powerful minister, Cardinal Richelieu, was the founder of Quebec and the governor of New France. He was a very important explorer of the St. Lawrence, Saguenay, Ottawa and Oneida river systems, and he had many contacts with the Huron, amongst whom he lived for a time. He helped to finance his work by assuring the French that there was certain to be a passage through this new country to Asia.

Henry Hudson (active 1607-1611), Robert Bylot (active 1610-1616) and William Baffin (c1584-1622)

Henry Hudson was the first to sail up the Hudson River in New York in 1609. In 1610, in a ship called the *Discovery*, he sailed up the western coast of Greenland and into the second largest bay in the world, now called Hudson Bay in his honor. It was completely unknown until then. Hudson mapped much of its eastern shore under very difficult conditions. When he wanted to continue, his crew mutinied, setting Hudson and seven others adrift in a small boat. Their fate is unknown. Robert Bylot, one of the mutineers, managed the difficult feat of bringing the *Discovery* back to England. Bylot then returned on various trips on the *Discovery* to seek the Northwest Passage through Hudson Bay and the Arctic Islands. With him was William Baffin, the greatest navigator of his day, who was the first person to calculate longitude while at sea. Together Bylot and Baffin explored the Davis Strait — the passage between Greenland and Baffin Island — and the waters north of Baffin Island, discovering the Lancaster Sound, later understood to be the entrance to the Northwest Passage.

The Voyageurs (late 1600s-late 1800s)

The voyageurs were French fur traders who traveled the rivers of Canada and the northern United States in canoes trading for furs with the First Peoples. They were employed by commercial interests in Montreal and later by the Hudson's Bay Company. They knew the country well and served as guides for many explorers. In many cases they married Aboriginal women, and their children became known as Métis. The voyageurs' hard life involved many hours of canoeing and portaging heavy loads in harsh conditions under pressure of time.

Sieur de La Vérendrye (1685-1749)

La Vérendrye was a fur trader who traded north of Lake Superior. He became convinced that there was water not too far west — a western sea — that would be the route to Asia. In searching for that mythic sea, he and his sons explored as far west as North Dakota and the headwaters of the Missouri River before they realized that this river flowed south, not west. But in doing this they expanded the reach of the French fur trade into Manitoba.

Hudson's Bay Company, also known as the HBC (1670-present)

The oldest company in North America, the Hudson's Bay Company was founded by the British Crown to control northern and western Canada and serve the interests of the British. While it had rivals, both French and English, it was the dominant presence in the fur trade and served as a kind of government in the lands assigned to it by the Crown. Its most important post was York Factory on Hudson Bay. Much of the exploration of northern Canada and even the search for the Northwest Passage was undertaken by men working for the company. But for the company there was always a commercial motivation for these activities.

Henry Kelsey (1667-1724)

Kelsey was an important explorer of the plains. He played a key role in establishing the HBC's control over the northern land mass. He

was known for working well with First Peoples, which was useful in establishing commercial relations for the company.

Samuel Hearne (1745-1792)

Sent by the HBC to explore the Northwest Territories and the Coppermine River, Hearne made a close alliance with Matonabbee, a leading member of the Chipewyan people who was held in high regard by the Athabascan Cree. He was the first European to reach the Arctic Ocean by land and to see Great Slave Lake, but he did not believe that there was an east-west route to the Pacific. He wrote about the cultural ways of the tribes he met, and closely observed and recorded the habits of the animals of the northern plains.

George Vancouver (1757-1798)

Vancouver's great exploration of the Pacific Northwest was intended to counter Spanish claims that Spain controlled the whole Pacific coast of the Americas. Another motivation was to find the Northwest Passage, this time from the Pacific side. He traveled up the entire coast from Seattle to Alaska and mapped the challenging passages and inlets between the mainland and Vancouver Island with great accuracy.

Sir Alexander Mackenzie (1764-1820)

Mackenzie is best known for two remarkable feats of exploration under the North West Company, a rival to the HBC. First he went north on a river (now known as the Mackenzie River) to the Beaufort Sea. He had been instructed to go to Russia via this route. He traveled with First Nations people, going a distance of 3000 miles (4828 km) in 102 days. Having failed to reach the Pacific, he set out again. Following the advice of his First Nations guides he took what seemed an unlikely route and went down the turbulent Bella Coola River until he reached a First Nations settlement perched on stilts overlooking what was the Pacific. He became the first European to reach the Pacific by crossing North America on July 22, 1793.

David Thompson (1770-1857)

One of the great mapmakers, Thompson worked first for the HBC, but then moved to the North West Company, exploring the lands in the west. His major achievement was his mapping of the Columbia River from its source to its mouth in the Pacific. In so doing, he put up a post where the Columbia and Snake rivers meet, claiming the land for Great Britain and the North West Company. He was especially interested in those places where US and Canadian interests and borders were at stake.

Simon Fraser (1776-1862)

Working with the North West Company, Simon Fraser was sent into the Rockies to see if a new and more practical route to the Pacific could be found. While he did not find an easy way through the mountains, his explorations and establishment of Prince George and Rocky Mountain House, and his exploration of what is now known as the Fraser River were very important.

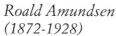

Sir John Franklin (1786-1847)

John Franklin was a British naval captain who fought in the Napoleonic wars. He was sent on a number of expeditions seeking the Northwest Passage by Sir John Barrow, second secretary of the British Admiralty, the man responsible for the great age of exploration. Franklin undertook expeditions by sea and by land, but he demonstrated serious weaknesses in his inflexibility, lack of physical strength and stamina, and perhaps a lack of ability to make successful contact with Aboriginal people. The story of his final expedition is told in this book.

Roald Amundsen (1872-1928)

Probably the greatest of all Arctic explorers, Amundsen, a Norwegian, was the first to traverse the whole of the Northwest Passage. He was also the first to reach the South Pole in 1911 and probably the first to reach the North Pole in 1926. He learned how to travel, eat and survive in the Arctic from Inuit.

Stan Rogers (1949-1983)

Born in Ontario, Rogers spent his summers in Nova Scotia. He played the guitar from the age of five and by fourteen was giving concerts. His songs were about Canada, its nature and the people who worked on the land and the sea — farmers, fishermen and sailors — as well as the poor. As a musician he traveled the country playing and singing in bars, folk clubs and festivals. Tragically, he died after the plane he was on caught fire upon landing. Rogers was helping others get off the plane when he died of smoke inhalation. He was one of Canada's best-loved musicians.

For Further Information

Listed below are a number of sources that I found invaluable in my research:

Arctic Passage, Nova DVD produced for PBS by the WGBH Science Unit (narration written by Chris Schmidt, produced and directed by Louise Osmond), 2006.
The stories of two Arctic voyages — the Franklin expedition and Roald Amundsen's navigation of the Northwest Passage. This source was especially useful concerning Inuit accounts of having seen members of the Franklin expedition in later years. See also the companion website at http://www.pbs.org/wgbh/nova/arctic/.

Dictionary of Canadian Biography Online, http://www.biographi.ca/index-e.html, ed. John English, University of Toronto and Université Laval, 2003.
An authoritative collection of biographies featuring people who have had a significant role in shaping the history of Canada.

Frozen in Time by Owen Beattie and John Geiger, Greystone Books, 2004.
The story of the Franklin expedition and anthropologist Owen Beattie's excavation and analysis of the three sailors buried on Beechey Island, and his hypothesis that tinned food led to their deaths.

Polar Exploration: The Heroic Exploits of the World's Greatest Polar Explorers by Beau Riffenburgh / The Royal Geographical Society, Seven Oaks, 2010.
Includes the stories of many famous adventurers such as Scott, Byrd, Shackleton, Amundsen and others, along with a rich array of period photos, maps and removable facsimiles.

Resolute: The Epic Search for the Northwest Passage and John Franklin, and the Discovery of the Queen's Ghost Ship by Martin W. Sandler, Sterling, 2008.
The remarkable story of the abandonment and discovery of one of the ships sent in search of the Franklin expedition.

Books of interest to younger readers:

A Dog Came, Too by Ainslie Manson, illustrated by Ann Blades, Groundwood Books, 1995.
A picture book tells the story of the big brown dog who accompanied Alexander Mackenzie and his First Nations guides on the trip overland to the Pacific Ocean.

Alexander Mackenzie: From Canada by Land by Ainslie Manson, Groundwood Books, 2003.
The story of the first European to cross North America by land and a fascinating glimpse into the early days of the fur trade in Canada.

Buried in Ice: The Mystery of a Lost Arctic Expedition by Owen Beattie and John Geiger with Shelley Tanaka, Scholastic/Madison Press, 1993.
The story of Sir John Franklin's search for the Northwest Passage and anthropologist Owen Beattie's investigation of the sailors buried on Beechey Island.

Kids Book of Canadian Exploration by Ann-Maureen Owens and Jane Yealland, illustrated by John Mantha, Kids Can Press, 2008.
A sweeping look at the history of exploration in Canada through the centuries.